A DAY IN THE WOODS

Created and photographed by Noel Keenan
Text by Val Clery

Designed by Nick Milton

BARRON'S

© Greey de Pencier Books, 1978. Printed in Canada

In a way, I'm sort of glad I'm on my own today – sometimes it's better to be in the woods by yourself. When I was little I used to think it was scary down here, but maybe any place is until you get to know it.

I bet even explorers felt a bit frightened coming through here the first time.

I wonder if this tree could have been here when the explorers were? Lucky that storms and lightning knock trees down – they make great bridges.

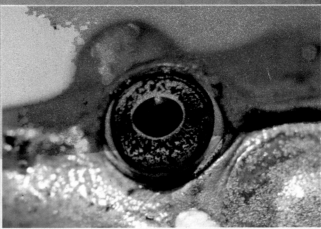

Uh huh, I've been spotted! But you're so clever, bullfrog, the way you hide under the duckweed with just your eyes showing like bubbles that I'm going to pretend I don't see you. I suppose you can look all around without moving, and if you spot any danger you're gone in a flash … and a splash!

Now here's someone who'd make a frog jump. It's too bad people are so scared of snakes. They're beautiful to watch …

What a big mouth you've got! Probably not big enough to eat a bullfrog, though, 'cause you garter snakes swallow your food whole. Imagine never chewing!

Hi, there! It looks like everybody's around today. So you're out showing off what a beautiful painted turtle you are? You really are, too, with that neat shell and those fancy pants and shirt – even if your mouth makes you look very old.

I wonder if dragonflies have mouths as fierce as dragons'?
They seem so harmless, but if you're a fly or mosquito about to
be eaten, dragonflies must seem ferocious.

Too bad they don't breathe fire…

Am I lucky today – a praying mantis, pretending to be a leaf. I hardly ever can find one of you, no matter how hard I try … it's easy to see how you got your name. And I'll bet you're praying I won't bother you…

All right, bumblebee, I don't want to disturb you either, I only want a closer look.

Now, ladybug, I know what you're looking for. Dad says you like aphids so he likes having you in the garden to eat them off his roses. Mom says it's lucky if you land on someone's hand, and you're just as pretty as that turtle back there, too.

Funny the way people like some kinds of insects and think others are creepy…

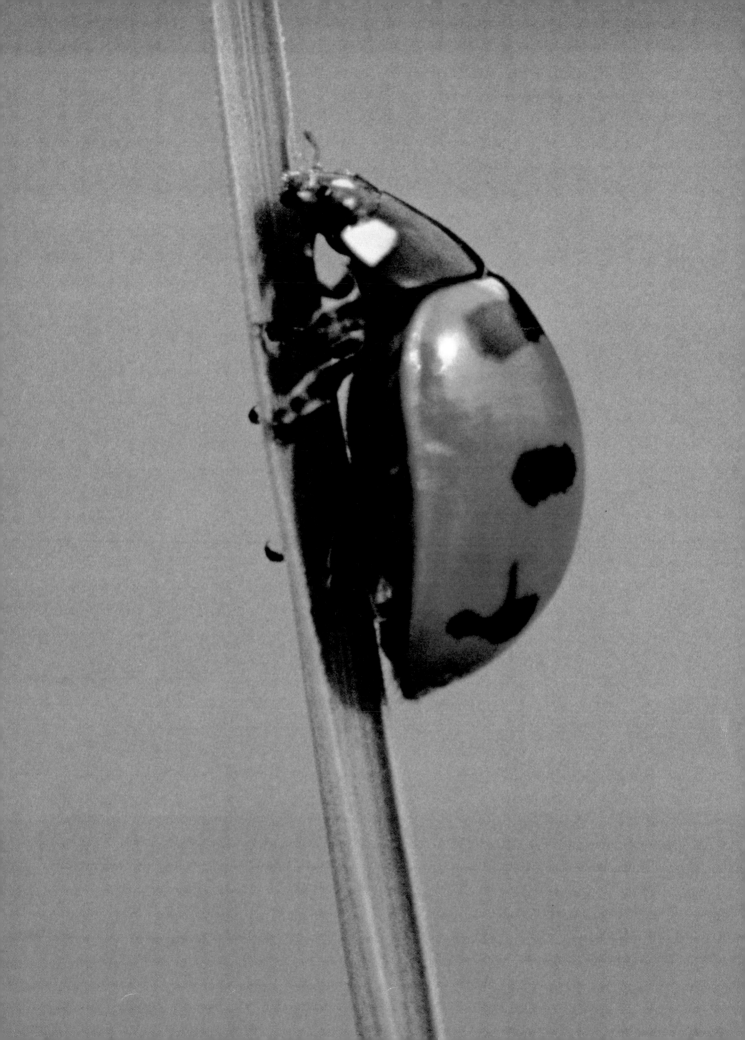

Like spiders...I think they're very smart! Even a machine couldn't make a web as fine as this. And the way a spider puts it all together – swinging down from twigs, spinning the threads as it goes and sticking them all in just the right place. It's not fair the way some

people go round breaking spiders' webs. After all that hard work.
    Hmm, here's one that's caught her dinner. That grasshopper is bigger than she is, but just the same she's got it all tied up. I guess she's waiting till she's hungry.

Oh, look … black-eyed Susans … they always make me think of Grandma and that song she used to sing whenever she saw them.

Hey, look at this inchworm – you look ready to march in a parade with your matching boots and cap …

And you, snappy dresser, with that antenna you look as though you've got a CB radio. *Got your ears on, good buggy?*

Uh huh, what's that up there? Better watch out, bugs … here comes the air force!

If only I'd brought the bird book. That one over there is a
flicker, I think. It hasn't got a moustache…
so maybe it's a female …
but whichever it is,
it'll be down here
having a snack of ants
as soon as I go away…
so look out, ants!

This bright red one I remember
for sure – a scarlet tanager, up north for the summer.

He sounds a bit like you would,
robin, if you had a sore throat.
Now, I wonder where my best
friend in the woods is?
Usually he's around here
somewhere …

And if I go very softly…

Hi, Fluffy! Aw, come on down, don't be shy. You remember me ... how I looked after you when that dog killed your mom? Come on and we'll go for a walk.

Dad was right, y'know, Fluffy. It was nice having you as a pet, but you need to live here in the woods. I miss you a lot sometimes, but you're still my friend, aren't you?

Here, Fluffy, here's a treat. Wild strawberries, look. We'll take them down to the water ... Y'know, I just read that some people call raccoons like you wash-bears, because when you're playing in the water it looks as if you're washing your food with your paws. Mom's still saying to me, "Why don't you wash your hands like Fluffy used to?"

… Say, if we had a swim now, I wouldn't need a bath tonight. Come on Fluff, paddle harder. No one ever had to teach you how to swim, did they? And you can go in the water without taking your clothes off.

There you go, Fluffy, you know your way home from here. I'll be back to see you soon, I promise. Now you look after yourself and get up a tree fast if you hear any dogs around.

I sure do hope nothing ever happens to Fluffy. I want him to be here always. I'm going to miss him when winter comes, but he'll remember me in the spring. Only he'll be bigger, and so will I, a bit …

Wonder what time it is? Mom said she'd keep dinner, but I'd better get going anyway …

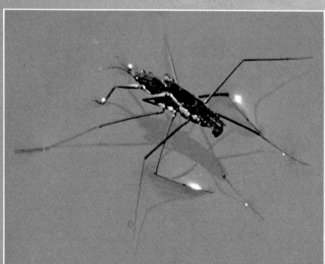

Still, it's so nice just to slosh along when you're hot and tired. But it'd be even better if I could skim along like those water striders, too. Then I'd be home in no time at all.

What a great day! Every time I come through these woods I see something new and I bet if I could come every day until I was old I'd still be finding out things. I wish sometime I could sleep down in the woods. I'd take the tent, light a fire and cook stuff. And maybe Fluffy could be there too, in case I got lonely.

Mom! I'm back, Mom!

Did you keep some dinner?

The boy shown in A Day In The Woods is Rory Keenan, who lives in Ontario, Canada close to the woods you have seen in this book. The photographs were all taken by Rory's father, Noel Keenan. As you probably know, it takes a lot of care and patience to photograph insects, reptiles, animals and birds close up. So it took many days over two summers to photograph all the scenes in this book, and of course Rory's father had to take many, many more pictures than you have seen here. Rory really did look after the young raccoon Fluffy when its mother was killed, and they did remain friends even when Fluffy was taken back to live in the woods.

Here is some more information about what Rory saw:

Duckweed is made up of millions of tiny water plants that float on the surface of a swamp or pond. Duckweed, not surprisingly, provides food for wild ducks and other waterfowl.

Bullfrogs are found in lakes, ponds and swamps in most parts of North America. They begin as eggs, after five to 20 days become tadpoles (greenish with black spots, with thick, long tails), and then they change into bullfrogs in one to three years, depending how warm a climate they live in. After three to five years they may have grown to 20 cm in length.

Their smooth skin is mottled green, but yellowish on the throat. They like to float just below the surface of the water, concealed by weeds, with only their eyes showing. They are strong swimmers and jumpers and eat fish, small snakes, even mice and young wildfowl; they are also quick enough to jump and catch flying insects. Their well-known croak sounds like *jug-a-rum*.

Garter (or Ribbon) Snakes of one species or another are found all over North America. They can be as short as 30 cm or as long as 1.5 m, and they have several yellow, brown or orange stripes down the length of their black, brown or dark green bodies. They eat earthworms, slugs, small frogs and minnows, and will sometimes go into the water after their prey. They swallow their food whole, yet they do have some teeth.

Painted Turtles are common all over North America, frequently living in swamps or along shallow, slow-moving streams. They range in length from 18 cm to 25 cm and their coloured markings vary from one subspecies to another. They love to bask in the sun on rocks or sandbanks. In the north they hibernate by burying themselves in mud or sand in water about a metre deep. They eat insects, snails, crayfish, small frogs and weeds, and they are hatched from eggs that the mother buries in sand near the water.

Dragonflies are born from eggs which may be implanted by the female dragonfly in the stalks of plants under water. After hatching they are called nymphs and live entirely under water, without wings, for almost a year.

They eat their own weight in tiny underwater creatures, fish spawn and worms every day. As they grow, a pair of wing pads forms on their backs to contain the new wings of the dragonflies developing inside. When the pads are quite large, the nymphs climb up plant stalks out of the water, then the skin rips open over the wing pads and dragonflies wriggle out. Dragonflies have very sharp eyes, made up of thousands of tiny lenses. They catch their food – mosquitoes, flies and moths – by forming their six legs into a basket shape and swooping on their prey, tearing the food with very powerful jaws.

Bumblebees usually make their colonies in abandoned mouse holes. A single queen founds the nest and lays all the eggs. The female worker bees collect nectar and pollen from blossoms and return it to the colony. Towards the end of summer, males and new queens are raised and leave the nest to mate. Before the first frost, the young queens hibernate under leaves or tree bark, but the old queen and her workers die in the colony.

Ladybugs are usually red with black spots and have wings folded under their shells. There are some 3,000 different species of ladybugs and almost all feed on aphids, which are harmful to plant life. So useful are ladybugs to farmers and gardeners that scientists have begun to breed them for pest control.

Praying Mantises (or Mantids) are to be found in most warm countries of the world. They are born from eggs hidden in a protective case of light, spongy fibre, about 4 cm long, that the female mantis attaches to a branch or twig. The mantis conceals itself in grass or among leaves and uses its powerful, sharp forelegs to catch flies, wasps, locusts, grasshoppers and other insects.

Spiders. The spiders shown are orbweavers, who weave nets to catch the flies, wasps and other insects they like to feed on. The webs or nets are made of silk that the spider produces from "nozzles" in its body. The silk threads can be made in different strengths and thicknesses and are smeared with a kind of glue that the spider also produces that prevents victims from escaping from the web. These spiders have poison fangs and when a fly or moth is caught, the spider immediately paralyzes it with a bite. When big insects, such as bees or grasshoppers, get caught, the spider first subdues them by binding them with more silk threads. Spiders have eight legs, each ending in curved claws that can grip the web and hold the victims.

Inchworms are the larvae of moths. Sometimes they are called "loopers" because of the way they loop their bodies up as they crawl, which they do because they only have feet at the front and back ends of their bodies. Some kinds of inchworms do serious damage to plants and crops.

Milkweed Beetles are just one of tens of thousands of kinds of beetles. As their name suggests, these like to live on milkweed, that tall, podded plant that looks so strange when it dries out in the fall.

Yellow-Shafted Flickers belong to the woodpecker family and, while they do peck nest-holes for their broods in rotten trees, they prefer to feed on the ground. Their favourite food is ants, which they dig out with their long beaks and trap with their long, sticky tongues. They usually migrate south in the winter.

Scarlet Tanagers also visit the north for the summer only, coming from as far away as South and Central America. They eat insects and tree grubs, moving rather slowly along the branches, and they sing like husky-voiced robins. The male birds turn green for part of the year.

Robins are probably the best-known birds in North America. They sing a lot, are very busy and aggressive and always hungry. They eat worms and insects and as much fruit as they can get. Their breast feathers are usually brick-red, sometimes mottled.

Raccoons are common throughout North America. Their coats are grey-brown with distinctive black bands around their tails. A black mask across their faces and eyes gives them the appearance of bandits, which they sometimes are if they can get into an orchard or chicken coop or garbage can. But they also like crayfish and freshwater clams and will go in the water to get them. They like to play in shallow water and because they sometimes play with their food in the water, people used to think that they were washing it. They sleep during the coldest days of winter in hollow trees, barns, garages and empty lofts, but can often be seen outside their dens on mild days.

Water Striders are also called gerrids, but water strider best describes the way they move across water on their four long, slender legs; they have two thicker, shorter forelegs that they use for catching food, usually small insects that have fallen into the water. Some gerrids have wings, but most do not.

Barron's Educational Series
113 Crossways Park Drive
Woodbury, New York

First U.S. Edition, 1978
ISBN 0-8120-5329-x